Great War Literature

NOTES

Written by W Lawrance

on

The Accrington Pals

A Play by Peter Whelan

Great War Literature Notes on The Accrington Pals a Play by Peter Whelan
Written by W Lawrance

Published by:
Great War Literature Publishing LLP
Forum House, Stirling Road, Chichester PO19 7DN
Web site: www.greatwarliterature.co.uk
E-Mail: enquiries@greatwarliterature.co.uk

Produced in Great Britain

Copyright © Wendy Lawrance 2004 - 2013.
The moral right of the author has been asserted.

ISBN 978-1905378180 (1905378181) Paperback Edition

All rights reserved: no part of this publication may be reproduced, stored in a retrieval system, or transmitted in any form or by any means, electronic, mechanical, photocopying or otherwise, without the prior written consent of Great War Literature Publishing LLP.

Great War Literature Publishing LLP reserve the right to amend this document without any prior notification.

This study guide is sold subject to the condition that it shall not, by way of trade or otherwise, be lent, re-sold, hired out or otherwise circulated without the publisher's prior consent in any form of binding or cover other than that in which it is published and without similar conditions being imposed on the subsequent purchaser.

Design and production by Great War Literature Publishing LLP
Typeset in Neue Helvetica, ITC Berkeley Old Style and Trajan Pro

Great War Literature Notes on

The Accrington Pals
a play by Peter Whelan

CONTENTS

Preface	5
Introduction	7
Synopsis	9
Act One	9
Act Two	16
Characters	21
May Hassal	21
Tom Hackford	24
CSM Rivers	26
Minor Characters	27
Historical Significance	29
History of the Accrington Pals	29
The Battle of the Somme	31
Themes	35
Sacrifice	35
Changing Times	37
Relationships	39
Comparisons	41
Effects of War	41
Portrayal of Women	43
Faith	45
A Question of Comparisons	47
The Changing Role of Women	47
Portrayal of Friendships in War	48
Further Reading	51
Bibliography	55
Other Titles	57

GREAT WAR LITERATURE NOTES

Preface

Great War Literature Study Guides' primary purpose is to provide in-depth analysis of First World War literature for A-Level students.

Great War Literature Publishing have taken the positive decision to produce a more detailed and in-depth interpretation of selected works for students. We also actively promote the publication of our works in an electronic format via the Internet to give the broadest possible access.

Our publications can be used in isolation or in collaboration with other study guides. It is our aim to provide assistance with your understanding of First World War literature, not to provide the answers to specific questions. This approach provides the resources that allow the student the freedom to reach their own conclusions and express an independent viewpoint.

Great War Literature Study Guides can include elements such as biographical detail, historical significance, character assessment, synopsis of text, and analysis of themes.

The structure of Great War Literature Study Guides allows the reader to delve into a required section easily without the need to read from beginning to end.

The Great War Literature Study Guides have been thoroughly researched and are the result of over 30 years of experience of studying this particular genre.

Students must remember that studying literature is not about being right or wrong, it is entirely a matter of opinion. The secret to success is developing the ability to form these opinions and to deliver them succinctly and reinforce them with quotes and clear references from the text.

Great War Literature Study Guides help to extend your knowledge of First World War literature and offer clear definitions and guidance to enhance your studying. Our clear and simple layouts make the guides easy to access and understand.

GREAT WAR LITERATURE NOTES

Introduction

First performed in 1981, this play tells of the formation, service and eventual decimation of the Accrington Pals, one of many such battalions founded as a result of Kitchener's call to arms in 1914.

Interwoven with this story of a town's loss, is the personal story of two of its characters. One is an individualist, a young woman seeking to make her own way in the world, not to rely on others, but to take responsibility for her own future. The other is an idealist, a believer in the collective good. He thinks that everyone has a duty to take care of their fellow man.

This unlikely couple form a friendship, which slowly and falteringly blossoms into romance. It is their misfortune to have met at a time when personal beliefs and feelings had to take second place to the nation's needs - which cost the lives of so many.

Pals marching through Accrington centre before they received their uniforms.
(Image Ref: WT400)
Image courtesy of William Turner Collection, Lancashire County Library and Information Service

The Accrington Pals
A play by Peter Whelan

Synopsis

ACT ONE

SCENE ONE

It is Autumn 1914 and Tom Hackford enters, pulling a green-grocer's cart and begins to get it ready for the early-morning customers. He is joined by May Hassal, who seems surprised that Tom has managed to get out of bed at all. After a while, May mentions Tom's behaviour the previous night, to which she has clearly taken some offence. It would seem that Tom had returned home very late and quite drunk. May believes that she heard Tom call out that he would be glad to go away, to be free of her. Tom tries to assure May that she misheard him: he had really said that he would be glad to be away from the town. May's anger eventually subsides, although it is clear that she disapproves of him enlisting, believing it to be a waste of his life.

They are interrupted by the arrival of Arthur Boggis. He is going around the streets, waking up the mill-workers [a knocker-up was often employed by the factories to ensure that their workers woke up and got to work on time]. This is not normally Arthur's job, but he is covering for another man who is unwell. He stops for a short chat before passing on. Then his son, Reggie arrives, announcing that he has been out all night and is trying to avoid his mother, who will be angry with him. Reggie leaves again and Tom's friend Ralph enters. He seems to think that Tom will have asked a favour of May, but it would appear that Tom has not yet had the opportunity. Eva Mason arrives and an embarrassing scene ensues: Tom should have asked May if Eva could take over his job on the stall, and his room in May's house. May is, however, unaware of this and both she and Eva feel awkward, but May quickly agrees that Eva can stay, although she is angry with Tom for not mentioning the situation beforehand.

Reggie's mother, Annie Boggis appears in search of her son, followed by one of the mill-workers, Sarah Harding. Reggie approaches his mother, who is extremely angry with him. Another mill-worker, Bertha Treecott, enters and, while she and Sarah wait for their fruit, they comment on the domestic argument unfolding before them. Eva is quite shocked by Annie's violence, but the others explain that this is quite normal behaviour. Everyone is relieved when the factory hooters sound to mark the beginning of the working day.

Later, Eva and May are alone, clearing away the stall and discussing the men who have enlisted. Eva is supportive of their decision, but May believes that the unemployed should have gone first. Eva is keen to stay with May and help on the stall, although, as May points out, times are hard and she can barely make ends meet. They briefly talk about Eva's relationship with Ralph, which May seems to believe might be closer than Eva admits. May gives Eva a less than favourable account of life in the town and it becomes apparent that May is ambitious to better herself. Eva reminds May that she will miss Tom and that she had gone to the recruiting office to plead for him not to have to go to the war.

SCENE TWO

This scene depicts May's memories of her visit to the recruiting office where she met Company Sergeant Major Rivers, to whom she had appealed for Tom's release from military service. She had tried very hard to make Rivers see things from her perspective - explaining how young and impressionable Tom is and that he was goaded into joining up: she had even offered to pay Rivers for Tom's release. The CSM had been unyielding: Tom had signed on and was keen to do his bit. He had politely suggested to May that she should concentrate on running her business and leave Tom's welfare to the army. May had eventually been forced to accept that there was nothing more she could do and had left, disappointed.

SCENE THREE

Back in the present, Bertha, Sarah and Eva are standing by the stall discussing the way the local men have changed since they joined-up. Bertha says that she wishes she could do more to help with the war effort, although Sarah believes the war will be over before the men have even completed their training. They are joined by Ralph and Bertha relates a story she has read in the newspaper about German atrocities in Belgium. Tom arrives and Ralph reminds him that he had promised to draw a sketch of Eva, so Tom promptly begins a drawing. The Boy's Brigade band can be heard in the background, ready to see the troops off. Reggie and his parents enter, and as ever, Annie is scolding her son because he should be playing with the band, but is running late. Arthur is in uniform, ready to depart with all the other men and is carrying one of his prized homing pigeons, named England's Glory. He is planning to take the bird with him to France. He suggests that they should all join together and say a prayer.

The time has come for the men to go to the station, but May, who had arrived quietly a few minutes earlier, refuses to go and see them off. Everyone departs, leaving Tom and May alone. He suggests that he could find an excuse not to go, but May is still too angry with him to really acknowledge this. She offers him some money, which he refuses. An awkward silence follows before Tom tries to embrace May. She rejects him forcefully and he leaves, angry at her cold attitude.

SCENE FOUR

Time has moved on and it is now winter. Eva and Sarah sit in May's kitchen while Eva reads a poem from the local newspaper. Sarah is concerned that May will be angry to find her sitting in the kitchen, but then remembers that May will be late because she will have gone to Peel Park to sell goods to the upper-class ladies who live there. Eva admits that she misses Ralph and the two women are happily enjoying their chat when May returns. Much to Sarah's surprise, May is not angry, but seems to be in a much better mood than the other two had expected. While she makes the tea, May reveals that she has received a letter from Tom, which appears to be the cause of her cheery mood. Sarah leaves and May and Eva discuss Eva's day at work. Then May divulges that she has been looking at premises, with a view to expanding her business. She recalls her upbringing and her family's fall from prosperity. While they are both in a confiding mood, Eva lets slip that she and Ralph have slept together. May is surprised, but not unduly shocked and they then move on to the topic of her and Tom. May denies that she has any feelings for Tom and quickly changes the subject again. She tells Eva that one of her upper-class customers, a Mrs Dickenson, has shown an interest in hearing Eva sing at one of her charity concerts. May seems keen that Eva should perform as it will advance her own reputation. They both look forward to the men coming home on leave, although May anticipates that Tom will go to his aunt in Salford.

SCENE FIVE

Tom is on guard duty at the training camp. He is joined by CSM Rivers who gives him some advice about being on guard. They then discuss May for a short while until Rivers turns the conversation around to comradeship and loyalty, reminding Tom that others are relying on him to do his duty and not let them down.

SCENE SIX

Tom and Ralph are on leave. Ralph and Eva are upstairs while Tom and May sit in the kitchen, trying to hide their embarrassment at the obvious antics which are taking place in Eva's bedroom. May seems surprised that Tom has chosen to spend his leave with her, rather than his aunt. He does not really answer this, but instead begins to praise the army for its ability to allow the men to function without money. He sees it as a fair exchange that a man should get his board and lodging in return for the use of any skills he might have. May perceives this ideology as naive. As they move closer, however, May becomes nervous and when Tom tries to take her hand, she once again rejects him. Just before she leaves the room, she asks Tom to draw a picture of her before he goes back to the camp. They embrace and May wishes that they were meeting now for the first time, with Tom as a man, rather than the innocent boy she recalls from his first arrival.

SCENE SEVEN

Arthur has written a letter home to Jack, the man he had replaced on knocking-up duty. Arthur reveals that the battalion has moved to Ripon. This letter shows Arthur as a very religious man, who seems to feel that the war is God's way of cleansing the earth of its sins.

SCENE EIGHT

Time has moved on and it is the winter of 1915. Sarah, Bertha and Eva, at the stall, discuss Bertha' new job as a tram conductress. Bertha says that the men that she works with do not treat her very well. Eva thinks this is because the men are frightened of women taking over their jobs. A minor disagreement follows as Eva tries to defend the men, while Sarah takes the side of the working women. This is broken up by the entrance of Annie Boggis, who is, once again, searching for Reggie. Sarah and Annie argue over Annie's behaviour towards her son and she gleefully tells them that she has discovered that the men are being sent to France. May, who had discreetly entered during the argument, confirms that this is true. Sarah and Bertha go, followed by Annie. Eva is worried about Ralph and May tries to reassure her, while blaming herself for having been so harsh to Tom.

SCENE NINE

It is a few weeks later and Tom and Ralph are once again on leave. Ralph is taking a bath in the kitchen, while Tom mends a pair of May's shoes. Eva joins them and helps Ralph, although her presence obviously makes Tom feel uncomfortable. When May returns, there is an awkward scene, although Tom reassures her that nothing improper had happened as he had been present. May, in an effort to be more friendly to Tom, praises his work on her shoes and he goes off to borrow some wax from a neighbour. May tells Eva that she has brought a rabbit home for their dinner. Ralph offers to skin the rabbit in return for being allowed to share it with them. May agrees and while Ralph is doing this, tells Eva that she is confused about her feelings for Tom. Eva assures her that Tom is in love with her. Although May is still unsure, she is clearly flattered and begins to wonder how matters will progress, when Tom enters with Reggie, who is bleeding. They all attend to him and when he is more calm it becomes clear that he has had a fit. They also learn that his mother had hit him with the buckle end of a belt.

May seems less willing than the others to help Reggie: she is worried about how Annie might react to any interference. May speaks to Reggie and tells him to say to his mother that he is now working for May on the stall. Reggie leaves and is quickly followed by Tom, who is unhappy at May's actions. There is an angry exchange between them before Tom departs. Although she is initially reticent, May goes after him to persuade him to come back.

SCENE TEN

Outside, May looks around for Tom, only to come face-to-face with CSM Rivers. He tells May that Tom has already left for the station. He speaks of the pride which the men have in their home town and in each other. May is angry and leaves.

Main Points of Interest in Act One

THE CHARACTERS
- All of the main characters are introduced early in Act One. The audience learns about their backgrounds and opinions on various matters.
- May's and Tom's characters are fleshed out, and their faltering relationship begins to show signs of blossoming, although their different attitudes always seem to come between them.

THE PALS
- The men display different perspectives and reactions to having enlisted, and towards the war in general. Once they have departed for France, however, they seem more bored than anything, although they have not really seen any action yet.
- The women also have different points of view about their menfolk joining up. These range from Eva's fear for Ralph's safety, to May's anger at the waste of valuable young lives.

WORKING WOMEN
- All of the women featured in the play are working. Some of them, as the story progresses, take on positions vacated by the men who have gone to fight.
- The women show different reactions to their new role in society and the changes which taking place in their lives.

ACT TWO

SCENE ONE

IThis scene opens with Ralph, now in France, reading a letter which he has written to Eva. It is just before the beginning of the Battle of the Somme and Ralph has written this letter as a confession to Eva, although he does not believe she will ever receive it. In this letter, as well as describing how he feels about the anticipated attack, he also admits to having slept with some prostitutes while he has been away. He feels guilty about this and wishes he could be at home with Eva.

Back in May's kitchen, Eva is sewing her outfit for the charity concert. May comes in, tired and hot from doing her deliveries in Peel Park. Eva had been planning to go to the pub with Sarah and Bertha, but May announces that she has invited the others round to her house. Both women are in the mood for a celebration as they believe that the battle which is about to start in France will bring about the end of the war. May is feeling extra cheerful because she thinks she has found a shop which she could take over. Much to Eva's surprise, May suggests that they become partners in the new business venture. Eva is concerned, however, that May only wants her to be involved because she will eventually marry Ralph and then Tom will also come back. May is hurt by this accusation which she feels is unfair.

SCENE TWO

Tom reads a letter which he has written to May. He thanks her for the food parcel she had sent to him and tells her about the comradeship between the men. He has done some sketches of his friends and has enclosed these with his letter. He tells her that he is trying to draw a picture of her from some photographs which he has.

SCENE THREE

The four women are enjoying their get-together in May's kitchen. They are singing, dancing and drinking beer. Sarah announces that Bertha has a boyfriend who is an asthmatic electrician. Because of his illness he has failed his medical examination and been unable to enlist. Bertha says that, despite his attentions, she could never love a man who had not gone to fight. Eva, Bertha and Sarah talk about their men, but May's attitude becomes harsh: she disapproves of the way women conduct themselves. She suddenly realises how drunk she is and excuses herself. As Sarah and Bertha prepare to leave, they discuss with Eva how strained her relationship with May has become lately.

SCENE FOUR

The scene changes to the trenches, just before the attack. Ralph and Tom are together and, while Ralph adjusts his pack and talks about the forthcoming attack, Tom ponders about workers' rights and who should lead them. As they are ordered to get ready, Ralph becomes nervous. Arthur, who is also with them, talks to his pigeon. CSM Rivers joins the men, with last-minute advice - paying special attention to Tom. Arthur seems to have lost his faith in God, as his prayer no longer praises God, but blames Him for what has happened. As they go over-the-top, the scene changes and the audience sees Eva singing at the charity concert. She forgets the words of her song and runs off the stage - angry with herself.

SCENE FIVE

Sarah is in her back yard, hanging out washing when Annie appears, looking for Reggie, who eventually arrives. Annie is cross with her son for telling rude rhymes to some of the local children. Bertha runs in carrying the local newspaper and shouting that the war is over. May and Eva join them and Sarah reads from the newspaper. The women are all delighted and relieved: they start celebrating. May takes the newspaper and reads an article about the charity concert. It would seem that Eva's mistake has been interpreted as her becoming over-emotional during the singing of such a patriotic song. May is pleased by this and while they discuss it, Annie notices a pigeon approaching, which she believes to be England's Glory - the bird which Arthur had taken to France. Initially, the others try to convince her that the bird could not have found its way back from France, but she remains certain. Eva agrees to fetch the pigeon so they can check whether it is carrying a message, but they find nothing and Eva takes it away. Annie becomes hysterical in her belief that this must mean that Arthur is dead. Reggie arrives and takes his mother home, as she is becoming more and more distraught.

SCENE SIX

In May's kitchen, Eva acts out Ralph's bath again - she obviously believes that he too is dead. May enters and chastises her friend for this behaviour. She shows Eva a newspaper report where there is no mention of the Accrington Pals having suffered great casualties and hopes that this will quell Eva's fears. The two women argue and Eva goes to strike May, who angrily tells her to leave.

SCENE SEVEN

Reggie is helping May on the stall. She enquires about his mother, who it would seem has suffered a complete breakdown. May tells him to go home and look after Annie. Bertha arrives, looking for Sarah. The two women have been trying to glean more information about the casualties. Sarah suddenly appears and tells the others, including Eva, who has just arrived, that there are only seven of the Pals left alive. They agree that they should all march to the town hall the next morning to discover the truth from the Mayor. May disagrees and Eva leaves her.

Once alone, May begins to believe that she can see Tom. She says that she is not afraid but she wants to know whether or not he is dead. CSM Rivers appears to her and says that he is looking after Tom and that over 100 men survived - not seven as the women believed. May asks to use his rifle and he shows her how. As she takes aim, Tom appears in the shadows before her and she shoots him. He does not fall, however, because he is already dead. Rivers tells May how Tom died: heroically defending his friends. May is distraught that Tom has thrown away his promising life. Rivers tells Tom that it is time for them to go. May is now so sorry and reaches out to Tom who touches her hands before passing on his way.

SCENE EIGHT

May and Reggie are at the stall, although May seems to be in a dream-like state - not really aware of what is happening around her. Eva enters, carrying her suitcase. She is leaving to go to her sister, who needs help. May is sad to see her friend go, but refuses to accompany her to the bus stop. She asks Eva to read a poem from the newspaper, which she does with some reluctance. Eva then leaves May and Reggie, who return to their work on the stall.

Main Points of Interest in Act One

DEVELOPING RELATIONSHIPS
- The relationship between Eva and May begins to show signs of disintegrating. Their differences are becoming more obvious - especially with regard to the fate of the men in France.
- May is secretly worried about Tom and after the news from France begins to look very bad, he appears to her, in spirit form. She blames herself for what has happened to him.

REACTIONS TO THE NEWS
- When the news appears to be good, the women celebrate. However, as the truth comes to light, Annie - who had always seemed a harsh woman - reacts badly. She suffers a breakdown once she believes that her husband will not be returning.
- Many of the women join together to march to the town hall and discover the truth about the men. This is the sort of collectivism of which Tom would have approved. May, however, declines to take part - she will find out on her own.
- Once they have discovered the truth, the main female characters react differently: Eva is angry, while May seems to be in a trance - initially unable to function in her normal way. The poem which May wants to hear speaks of pride at the deaths of the town's men - which is not how May had felt before.

CHARACTERS

MAY HASSAL

May appears to be a harsh, strong woman, in her late twenties or early thirties. Her background is very different from the life she now leads and one of her main priorities is to better herself; to regain some of the status which her family had previously held. She knows that most of the other characters do not really like her, but she is not too worried by this, as she has no intention of standing still - she wants to move on in the world. She has little patience for those who lack ambition, or for others who dream their lives away, rather than getting on with things.

May's upbringing has a great impact on her attitude. Her family had been fairly well-to-do, until her father had lost his job and set in motion their downfall. It is clear that May views herself as a cut above the girls who work in the mill and it is this sense of superiority whch fuels her ambition to escape her current surroundings.

One of May's strongest characteristics is her fierce sense of independence. She believes that women should be treated in the same way as men, especially as they are taking on so much of the men's work. May has set high standards for herself, but she also seems to expect others to behave with the same decorum as she exhibits. Every so often, however, she lets her guard down and it becomes clear that many of her actions and opinions are actually a cover for the real May, who seems to be quite lonely. Despite her bravado, she appears pleased to have Eva's company and is genuinely sorry when Eva has to leave.

May's relationship with Tom is far more complex. He is ten years younger than May and, although this does not seem to bother him, she feels that this age-gap is a major stumbling block in their relationship. Although, on the surface, May seems not to care about Tom, especially at the beginning of the play, this is clearly not the case. She had gone to the recruiting office to try to persuade the authorities to refuse Tom's enlistment and she seems to resent the fact that he is leaving her. When he comes home on leave for the first time, she warms to him, but ultimately he is once again rejected. Her admission here is interesting as it would appear that she is held back by her memories of how immature Tom had been when he first arrived. She wishes that they were meeting now for the first time.

During Tom's next leave, however, May decides that she will take the initiative and decides to suggest that he should sleep with her. Nevertheless, circumstances prevent this from happening and they part angrily.

May's attachment to Tom is made more complicated by her feelings of guilt. She feels reponsible for him while he is alive and, having pushed him away, she feels as though she is to blame for his death. This is demonstrated most particularly in Act 2, Scene 7 which is a dream-like re-enactment of Tom's death, during which it is May who shoots him. May seems to have conflicting emotions about Tom; rejecting him one minute, then reacting angrily when she feels he is being critical of her, and this confusion may be a reflection of the times through which they are living. For the women in the play, their lives are undergoing great upheavals as they come to terms with the changes brought about by the war. With the exception of the ladies who live at Peel Park, most of the women work and their roles in society and the workplace are changing. May's independence and ambition cause others to wonder about her motives and although she clearly loves Tom, it is equally clear that she will allow nothing to stand in the way of her own progress. This might seem like a harsh attitude, but many women began to question traditional values and re-evaluate their position in society during the First World War.

Despite the fact that May has ambitious plans for the future, her feet are firmly on the ground. She is realistic about her relationship with Tom, anticipating that their age-gap might cause problems. She also understands the social strata and realises that, only by her own hard work, will she be able to better herself. She keeps her head when all the others believe the rumours about the number of dead and, while they march to the town hall demanding answers, she remains behind. Once she is alone, however, she gives in to her own fears which demonstrates that, at least some of her actions take the form of a performance for the benefit of the others. In reality, she is desperately worried about Tom, but she refuses to let the other women see a chink in her armour, believing that this would be a sign of weakness. In addtion, May refuses to act collectively - she prefers to find things out for herself, rather than join with others. This shows her independence, but also reflects her rejection of Tom's stance on the power of acting as a group with a shared goal, rather than as individuals.

May's attitude to the charity concert is also interesting. She is keen for Eva to participate, despite her new friend's reluctance, because she believes it will enhance her own reputation within the community. Her willingness to fawn to the ladies at Peel Park shows another of the complexities of May's character. She believes in her own independence and superiority, but knows that she must nurture the upper-class ladies if she wants her business to prosper. This sort of contradictory character trait comes across in May's personality throughout the play, as she hides her emotions from everyone, sometimes even herself. This is demonstrated particularly well in her relationship with Tom, which lacks the intimacy shared by Eva and Ralph. On the one hand May obviously has a lot of self respect and refuses to 'give' herself to a man, yet believes that, due to their age gap, she would be ruining *Tom's* life, rather than her own, if they were to be together.

May is a very private person, who keeps herself to herself and expects others to do likewise. She does not interfere in other people's lives and does not appreciate it if they pry too much into her affairs. Her aloof attitude makes her unpopular amongst the other working girls and eventually drives a wedge between her and Eva.

Tom's death has a great impact on May. She becomes more introspective, examining her own role in Tom's life and death. She feels guilty for allowing him to go to the war and for rejecting his affections, but she is also angry that he went to fight in the first place. Following his death, May seems to fall into a dream-like state, hardly aware of what is happening around her. She appears to have lost her ambition and her high opinions of herself, along with her hopes for the future, settling back into her old life and making do.

TOM HACKFORD

At the beginning of the play, Tom is a 19-year-old apprentice who lodges at May's house and has done since before her father died. He helps May with the fruit and vegetable stall, although he has recently joined up and, like the other new recruits, is about to start his training. May refers to him as a dreamer, which is how he seems to her, but this reflects her attitude, rather than his. May believes that people have to help themselves, while Tom has more faith in collective good: that people, acting as a group, are stronger and can ensure a better standard of living for everyone. His ideas are, however, somewhat impractical, given his situation, and this fuels May's argument that he is being unrealistic.

Tom does not see himself as a leader, but goes along with the others. He enlists with his friends, gets drunk with his friends and eventually dies with them too. Despite this, his beliefs are so strong that one can imagine him turning to a life in politics or social reform, if he had survived the war. To him, his ideas are not dreams, but a realistic hope for a better, more equal, future for everyone.

Although May continually decries Tom's 'dreamy' opinions, he proves that he actually has quite a strong, mature and reliable character. He shows that he is good in an emergency when Reggie has a fit, by bringing him to May and trying to help, despite May's protests to the contrary. He feels uncomfortable at Ralph and Eva's open affection - finding it embarrassing to be present while they are carrying on. Finally, in the trench, before the men go over the top, he remains calm and Ralph looks to him for moral support.

Despite his youth, Tom is a proud man. He refuses to accept May's help or money. He seems to resent her offers of assistance, perhaps feeling that she is treating him like a child, when he really wants her to treat him like a man. In other ways, however, he is quite an innocent. His movements towards May, for example, are invariably awkward. This slight clumsiness might not be merely indicative of his youth: it might also demonstrate the strength of his feelings for May. He clearly loves her very much and wants to be with her, but is always unsure of her reactions. This insecurity, coupled with his obvious need for her, makes him behave even more awkwardly. He is in a difficult position in his relationship with May. Ordinarily, as the man, he would expect to take the lead. However, May's age and the fact that she is his landlady make him defer to her. His conduct is always 'gentlemanly', but his confusion over her reactions is obvious and this is hardly surprising, given how confused she is herself.

He thinks nothing of the age-gap between himself and May - in fact it never seems to enter his head that this might cause a problem for them. His occasional bitter outbursts towards May stem from her dismissal of his advances, or their disagreements over politics and society. Despite their differences and her rejection of him, he remains loyal and eager to please her. When he is on leave, rather than going to visit his aunt or going out with his friends, he mends her boots and is keen to impress her by doing the best job he possibly can.

Despite his belief that he is unsuited to the role of leader, Tom eventually proves that this is a task which he could easily have undertaken. When the men are in the trenches, he is the one with a clear head, showing a great deal of maturity in the face of almost certain death. In the final dream-like scene between May and CSM Rivers, it would seem that, in the final moments of his life, Tom had been overwhelmed by the injustice of his friends dying. He had struck out heroically against the enemy and, in doing so, had given his own life.

CSM RIVERS

Company Sergeant Major Rivers is a curious, yet vital character in the play. Appearing initially in May's imagination, as she remembers her visit to the recruiting office, he frequently crops up just at a point where either May or Tom are beginning to question their role within the war. At their first meeting, Rivers appears to May as the voice of officialdom, pointing out that Tom cannot retract his enlistment without a sound reason. He presents May with all sorts of reasons why she should allow Tom to do what he wants. He promises to take special care of Tom, which helps to assuage May's fears.

Rivers seems to know a great deal about May and Tom, although neither had met Rivers before. This gives his character a unearthly air, as though he is not quite real. He is self-assured and confident, but also kindly and considerate. Whenever he is present, he controls the scene and nothing that May says or does has any influence on him. This enhances his ethereal quality - it is like he is not really there, but merely part of May's or Tom's subconscience.

At the front line, he looks after Tom, giving him advice and encouragement. Although he asks after May, he is keen to remind Tom of his duty to his fellow soldiers and how much they are relying on him. Once Tom walks out of May's house, he appears, again almost from nowhere, to reassure May that Tom is doing the right thing. Whilst May is unconvinced by Rivers's arguments, nothing that she has to say changes his viewpoint. One could argue that Rivers represents May's conscience: deep down she knows that Tom must do his duty, despite her reluctance to accept this. He also seems to represent Tom's sense of duty, reminding him of his responsibilities and encouraging him before the battle.

Rivers's final appearance comes, once again, in May's imagination. He and Tom are both dead and he tries to reassure May that Tom died a hero, attempting to get to her accept Tom's death and the manner of it. Despite the presence of Tom's ghost, Rivers controls the situation, refusing to listen to May's protests that Tom has thrown away his life, or to condemn her for her perceived part in his death.

The proposition that Rivers is not a 'real' character is reinforced by the fact that Tom and May never talk about him. Whilst this does not give conclusive evidence as to the reality of his character, it is an indication that the role of Rivers could be interpreted as a subliminal one, helping the two main characters accept their situations and also assisting the audience in their understanding of the times.

MINOR CHARACTERS

As with most works of literature, the minor characters, while not necessarily vital to the plot, are there for a reason. In the case of *The Accrington Pals*, these less-involved personalities are used to demonstrate the various attitudes of people at that time. So, for example, Sarah and Bertha represent working-class women, whose lives are undergoing substantial changes due to the war. Sarah's marriage has never been happy, but she had previously accepted her lot in life. Now, as her role in society is having to change, she becomes more outspoken about her marriage and her husband. Bertha, on the other hand, has a different outlook. She is happy to take on the role of the men who have gone to war, but she still holds firm to her belief that it is a man's responsibility to fight and protect his homeland. She states that she could never love a man who had not done his duty.

Eva, as the newcomer, has most to learn about her new environment and her role changes throughout the play. Her involvement with Ralph shows how women's attitudes to sexual relations were changing. May's character represents a more repressed, conventioanl age, when women waited for marriage, while Eva believes in living for today, rather than waiting for something that might never happen. Her role within the workplace is representative of the inequality of the times. She carries out a man's work, but is not paid the same as a man would be and she also knows that when the men return, she will be expected to give up her job. Both she and May can see the injustice of this, but neither of them would really be prepared to act upon it.

The Boggis family seem fairly dysfunctional. Arthur appears to be a loner, enjoying the company of his pigeons and clinging to his faith. Annie is a hard woman, continually beating and reprimanding her son. She does not take kindly to criticism from the other women. Reggie is, initially, seen as a mischievous boy, whose sole purpose in life seems to be to annoy his mother. Their lives probably undergo the greatest changes as a result of their involvement in the war. Arthur completely gives up his faith in God, finding it hard to believe that the carnage which he is witnessing in France can be the work of a loving God. Annie suffers a complete breakdown when she hears of her husband's death, showing that she may have been more attached to him than anyone had previously thought. Reggie, who has never really had to be responsible for anything in the past, is forced to take over and become the head of the household.

Historical Significance

THE HISTORY OF THE ACCRINGTON PALS

When the First World War began on 4th August 1914, there was a general air in Great Britain, as in much of Europe, of patriotism and excitement. Almost immediately, Lord Kitchener was appointed as Secretary of State for War and his experiences in the Sudan and the Boer War made him believe that the forthcoming conflict was likely to be a long and costly one. He believed that a very large number of men would be required to defeat the German army and, as conscription was not politically acceptable at that time, he began a recruitment campaign to encourage the nation's men to volunteer. The government opened recruiting offices and army camps sprang up all over the country to train the new recruits.

Although the initial response was enthusiastic, the government and army continued to look for new ways to persuade young men to enlist. General Sir Henry Rawlinson, a senior army commander, suggested that men might be more inclined to join up if it could be guaranteed that they would know the men with whom they would be serving.

On 28th August, Lord Derby gave a stirring speech in Liverpool, urging local men to enlist together, to form a 'Battalion of Pals'. His call was answered and within ten days over 3,000 men had joined up, giving Liverpool not one, but three Pals Battalions. This achievement was widely reported in the press and, in towns and cities all over the country, local authorities applied to Lord Kitchener for permission to form their own Battalions of Pals. Some were made up of men who worked together, while others were formed from men who belonged to the same clubs or sports groups. In either case, however, especially in the battalions which were formed in the smaller towns, the men all lived in close proximity and were familiar with each other and their families.

In the Lancashire town of Accrington, there was a secondary incentive to enlist: the town was experiencing extreme hardship due to a decline in the cotton industry, upon which it traditionally relied. Men had been laid off and many families were suffering in conditions of severe poverty. The nationalistic fervour and desire to serve their country was fuelled by the financial benefit of a regular income from the army.

By 24th September a full-strength battalion had been formed from men in Accrington and the surrounding towns and villages. They began their training in nearby camps, before leaving for Caernarvon in February 1915. The battalion, whose official title was the 11th Battalion of the East Lancashire Regiment, remained at Caernarvon until May, when it was transferred to Penkridge Camp, near Rugeley in Staffordshire. Two more moves took place, firstly to Ripon and then to Salisbury, before the Accrington Pals received orders to leave for Egypt in December 1915. Their mission in Egypt was to fight the Turks and guard the Suez Canal, but their time there was short and they were posted to France in February 1916.

The commanders of the British and French armies had, by this time, already decided to launch a major offensive in the Somme area in the summer of that year. Initially, this was due to be a joint attack, but severe French losses at Verdun necessitated a change of plan and the Battle of the Somme became a mainly British operation: one in which many Pals battalions would partake.

The Accrington Pals were part of the assault on a hilltop fortress at Serre. Despite a week-long bombardment prior to July 1st, the attacking troops came up against heavy machine-gun fire on the first day of of the battle. Only a handful of men reached the enemy front-line trench and they were soon forced to retreat due to a lack of reinforcements. Of the 720 Accrington Pals who began the attack, only 136 were left when the battalion was relieved. The devastation of the Accrington Pals had taken less than half an hour.

The initial newspaper reports in Accrington stated that the battle was going well and that primary objectives had been taken. These optimistic accounts were soon replaced by growing lists of casualties and, as the reality became clear, the folly of sending men from the same area into battle together soon began to be evident. Almost every family felt the effects and the town, like many others, went into mourning for its lost sons.

Later, the battalion was brought back up to strength again and saw further service during the First World War before being disbanded in 1919. However, the comradeship which had epitomised the ethos of the Pals Battalions was lost forever, along with the men who had answered their country's call.

THE BATTLE OF THE SOMME

In late 1915, the Allies held a conference at Chantilly to the north of Paris. Here they decided that in 1916, major assaults would be made on all fronts, in an attempt to finally break down the German army. As part of this objective it was agreed that the French and British would combine on the Western Front in a major offensive at the point where their two armies met - the River Somme. The Commander in Chief of the British Army, General Sir Douglas Haig, preferred the idea of attacking further to the north, in Flanders, but was overruled by his opposite number in the French army, General Joseph Joffre. The French commander saw the forthcoming battle as one of attrition: his aim being to wear down the German army, rather than worry about making any signficant territorial gains.

In February 1916, while Haig and Joffre were still planning the anticpated attack, the Germans launched a massive offensive at Verdun. The German intention here was similar to Joffre's at the Somme - to wear down the French army, or as the German Chief of Staff, Erich von Falkenhayn is alleged to have put it, to "bleed France white". Falkenhayn had chosen to attack at Verdun because he believed that the French would defend this historic town to the last man, rather than cede it to the Germans. As French losses began to mount, Joffre demanded that the launch date for the Battle of the Somme should be brought forward from 1st August to 1st July 1916 in order to divert German resources from Verdun. In addition it was decided that the Battle of the Somme would have to become a predominantly British affair, with the French only participating in the south of the region. Joffre's preoccupation with defending Verdun meant that Haig now assumed responsibility for the planning of the Battle of the Somme.

Haig decided that the Fourth Army, under General Rawlinson, should lead the attack, although the two men initially disagreed as to the methods which should be employed. Haig favoured a speedy assault with little preliminary bombardment to maximise the element of surprise. Once the infantry had broken through, he intended to use his beloved cavalry to charge the German forces and turn the war back into a mobile one, rather than the stalemate it had become. Rawlinson, on the other hand, was an infantry man and preferred a more cautious approach, with a long bombardment followed by an infantry attack over a wider front, with a 'creeping barrage' being laid down by the artillery to protect the advancing troops. The two sides were never fully reconciled although Haig was forced to concede that a prolonged artillery attack was necessary in order to break down the strong German fortifications.

On 24th June the bombardment began, and continued until 1st July. The Germans had, however, built extremely strong defences and had occupied them for many months, thus ensuring that while the bombardment caused them great hardship, they survived - as did their front line. At 7.28am on 1st July, 17 mines were detonated along the front. Unfortunately, one of these mines exploded eight minutes earlier, giving the Germans advance notice of the impending attack. The men were ordered to go over the top at 7.30am and advance across No Man's Land at a walking pace. There were many reasons for this, including the general's misguided belief that the Germans and their defences would already have been destroyed by the artillery bombardment and that the men would find nothing but abandoned trenches awaiting them. In addition, Rawlinson was concerned that the New Army which formed the backbone of his force might begin to straggle once out in the open. In order for the 'creeping barrage' to work, the infantry must be kept together, rather than wandering off and risking being caught up in their own artillery fire.

Unfortunately, the barrage had failed in its aim of decimating the German defences and once the mines had exploded and the bombardment ceased, the German soldiers came out of their reinforced bunkers to man their machine guns. At the same time, the German artillery opened fire on No-Man's Land. The advancing British troops were an easy target, especially as much of the German barbed wire remained intact. While the bombardment may have failed to destroy its target, both it and the ensuing German artillery fire succeeded in severing the communication lines which had been laid down previously. This meant that the Generals behind the lines remained largely ignorant of what was taking place. Initial reports which filtered back to Headquarters were optimistic and orders were then issued which did not reflect the genuine requirements at the front. Reserves were sent to the wrong places and were, themselves, wiped out.

The date of July 1st 1916 is the bloodiest in British military history, and almost 60,000 men were either killed, wounded or reported missing on that day alone. Most of the men who went over the top that morning were the enthusiastic patriots of Kitchener's volunteer army, many of them from the newly formed Pals battalions. The men of the original British Expeditionary Force had effectively been wiped out in previous battles and, for many of the new recruits, the Somme was to be their first, and last, taste of battle.

The Battle of the Somme continued, despite these losses, and in one sense, one of Joffre's goals was achieved. The Germans were forced to transfer some troops and munitions from Verdun, which gave the French a welcome respite and allowed them to regain some control in that area.

By August, Haig had accepted that his hoped-for breakthrough was unlikely and the British concentrated on smaller actions while continuing to prepare for another 'big push'. This began on 15th September and is remembered mainly as the battle in which tanks made their debut. Haig had been a keen observer of the development of this new technology, but their impact was disappointing. Numbers were few, they were mechanically unreliable and in the cloying mud of the Somme, those that did not break down soon became stuck. The main achievement of the tank was to frighten the opposition. During this attack, despite the failure of the tanks, gains were made and it was deemed to have been a success, although once again, there was no great breakthrough.

As autumn approached, Haig continued to launch new offensives, hoping to break the German lines. However, the weather now worsened, turning the battlefield into a bog. Eventually the fighting in this area ceased near the end of November, leaving both sides to count the cost. Total Allied casualties during the battle were in excess of 600,000, with Germany losing roughly the same amount, although the figures were difficult to confirm. Germany's army had, until that time, been made up of regular soldiers, but would in future be compiled of conscripts and volunteers which, to a certain extent, made both sides more equal from then on.

Many historians have argued that Haig should bear responsibility for the massive losses incurred in the Battle of the Somme: that he should have ceased the attack once the level of casualties became clear. Others point out that he was bound by many restrictions, such as the political requirement to adhere to the wishes of the French Army; outdated war tactics and the need to fight a totally different type of war. These two opposing sides remain intransigent, each using selective reasoning and choosing to either ignore or dismiss any alternative to their own viewpoint.

What remains as an indisputable fact is that the Battle of the Somme and, in particular, its opening day, would become firmly etched in the mind of the British public, as the day when innocence was lost.

Pals relaxing at Rugeley Camp. (Image Ref: WT55-4)
Image courtesy of William Turner Collection, Lancashire County Library and Information Service

THEMES

SACRIFICE

This, together with the waste and futility of the conflict is a common theme in the literature of the First World War. *The Accrington Pals*, being a play about the decimation of a town and its people, features it perhaps more strongly than most. The fact that the men all come from the same place and many of them either live close together or work in the same places, heightens the sense of loss and sacrifice as the audience comes to understand the consequences of this method of recruiting when so many men are lost. It is not just the men who are called upon to make the 'ultimate sacrifice', but the whole town - including the women and children - whose lifes will never be the same again.

The central male character, Tom Hackford, is portrayed as a very young, idealistic, romantic man, who has a bright future and everything to live for. Tom's death symbolises the waste of the war and the indiscriminate nature of death.

By using an idealist as a central character, Peter Whelan is forcing the audience to question what might have been. If Tom had survived, for example, would he have gone into politics and become a leader of men. Would he have fulfilled all of his ambitions and did his sacrifice prove to be worthwhile. These are questions which remain unanswered because Tom has taken the decision to answer his nation's call and do his duty, and in doing so has sacrificed his life, and his hopes for the future.

Of all the characters in the play, the only one who senses the futility of the war is May. She realises that Tom might be throwing away his life and his ambitions and fails to understand the sense of duty which has driven him to enlist. Strangely, May also represents the antithesis of the idea of futility, as she sees the conditions brought about by the war as a good way to earn more money and enhance her business prospects.

A good example of the futile nature of the war can be seen in Ralph's letter to Eva at the beginning of Act Two. This scene follows Tom and May's argument and May's angry conversation with CSM Rivers, who has been pointing out the bravery of the men. In his letter, Ralph seems much less cheerful than normal. This may be because of his guilt over having slept with prostitutes, but there is also a sense of boredom and desperation. He speaks of waiting and being moved about a lot - all to no purpose. However, now he knows that there is a big battle ahead, he is unsure how he will face up to what he knows he must do. He also relates the conditions in the trenches and in No Man's Lane, indicating that this ground has been fought over before, but to no avail as the Pals are about to fight there again.

These themes are undercurrents which run throughout the play and which draw in the audience. This is made possible by the use of dramatic irony. The audience know that the first day of the Battle of the Somme cost many thousands of lives, but they also know that little ground was gained by these deaths and that the war dragged on for more than two years following the beginning of the attack which many characters in the play anticipate will be the final 'big push'. Many in the audience would also be familiar with the plight of the Pals battalions during that time. The characters are portrayed, quite accurately, as ignorant of their fate, which enhances the sense of a pointless sacrifice for the audience.

The scenes where the women discover the severity of the casualties also serve to highlight this theme. The initial estimate of seven survivors stuns the women and even the revised number quoted by CSM Rivers means that there would be hardly a single house in the town that remained unaffected by these catastrophic and costly losses.

CHANGING TIMES

The years immediately before and after the First World War saw great changes in society, class, status and attitudes. One of the most obvious of these was the change in the role of women. In *The Accrington Pals*, the women all have strong, forceful characters, most of them work in the mill and have done for many years. Until the war, they did not expect their lives to consist of anything but mill-work, marriage and children. With the war came new opportunities to undertake a different type of work, to travel more and to improve themselves.

May provides a good example of a strong, independent woman. She does not feel the need to have a man in her life and is happy to put all of her efforts into enhancing her business opportunities. She obviously feels that women are not as well treated as they should be, as she points out to Eva that the women are not as well paid as the men would be. Her interpretation of this is that if women continue to rely on men, they will always find themselves taking second place. May's fierce independence and distrust of others is behind these sentiments, but the facts are nonetheless true. Bertha's treatment on the trams provides another example of this inequality. Bertha has given up her job at the mill and gone to work on the trams. Once there, however, she discovers that the men feel threatened by the presence of women in their workplace. The women are not allowed into the rest room during their breaks and they are not paid as much as the men because they are, supposedly, not strong enough to do their work without assistance. This demonstrates the adjustments that both men and women were having to make and also how their attitudes varied. Eva, for example, seems to feel that her role is unimportant because she does not have to risk her life. Sarah, on the other hand, points out that the women working in the munitions factories are working in dangerous and unhealthy conditions.

The war placed women in a difficult social positiion. Their labour was required and, as the war progressed, it became a necessity, yet 'convention' still expected them to behave with due decorum. This was a new and awkward role for women, as their new-found independence gave them more freedom, but there were still restrictions on what was deemed to be acceptable behaviour. This gender confusion was enhanced by government propaganda and newspaper reports which portrayed men as heroes, going to war to protect their women from the German onslaught. Regardless of the accuracy of this statement, it is easy to see why both men and women found their new roles unclear. Men had traditionally been the bread-winners, but were now having to hand this role over to the women, who in turn became more independent, while being told that they still needed 'protecting'.

Another aspect of life and society that changed during the war was the attitude towards sex. In *The Accrington Pals*, this is best represented by May and Eva. May seems distant and inexperienced in her relationship with Tom, but as the war progresses, she mellows and softens towards him, even to the extent of contemplating suggesting that he sleep with her while on leave. This behaviour is out of character for May, but she has realised that her feelings for Tom are more intense than she had previously thought.

While, for May, an argument with Tom leaves this matter unsettled, Eva has already had sex with Ralph. Like many of her contemporaries, she is not prepared to wait for marriage. Sarah, for example, expresses her anger that the war didn't begin three years earlier, thus avoiding her having a child and getting married. Note, she doesn't say that she got married and had a child. Initially, sensing May's disapproval, Eva tries to keep the extent of her relationship with Ralph a secret, but eventually decides that she must be honest and reveals the truth. Although she tries to appear understanding, it is clear that May finds Eva and Ralph's situation difficult to accept.

Despite obvious encouragement from Tom, May continues to believe in self-control. Although there had always been men and women who didn't believe in the convention of waiting for marriage before having sexual intercourse, there was a marked increase during the First World War. Many reflected, like Eva, that to wait for an event that might never happen was pointless.

The war changed lives in other ways too. The Trade Union movement, which was still in its infancy, found many new followers, as represented by the character of Tom. He advocates the power of the collective voice and this reflects real changes that were occuring in social and political spheres. His friends find his attitude difficult to understand. To them his ideas seem unrealistic, as they have always accepted their lot in life. Linked to these changes was the blurring between different classes in society. In *The Accrington Pals*, May, who is always striving for a better social position, associates with the ladies of Peel Park, admiring their houses and clothes. She clearly aspires to be respected by them, while the other girls seem to think May has developed ideas above her station and is, in fact, demeaning herself. Sarah resents the upper-class ladies who become nurses - and the publicity which they seem to gain, while others, like Sarah, are working too.

RELATIONSHIPS

The Accrington Pals, being primarily a play about people, features their relationships and how their involvement in the war has great consequences. The main relationship in this play is between Tom Hackford and May Hassal. Having known each other for a few years, their friendship is already established. The most immediate effect of the war on their relationship is Tom's enlistment in the Pals battalion. May is unhappy at his going, although the reason for this is unclear. She seems to feel responsible for him, but in her own way, she also loves him. In addition, he is of great use to her in running the stall. Although her attempts to get CSM Rivers to release Tom from his commitment are unsuccessful, she resents his decision to join up. Tom's feelings for May are more clear. His affection for her increases throughout the play, although they are destined to be divided. Tom develops a deep sense of duty and despite the fact that he momentarily offers to remain with May, one instinctively knows that he will be go, because he must.

Tom and May's relationship is awkward, partly because of the age difference between them, but mainly because they have such different views and opinions. Their politics and social outlooks are poles apart. Tom dreams of a society in which people are treated equally and valued by others for their individual skills and abilities; May, on the other hand, firmly believes in the power of the individual and that men and women can only prosper through their own efforts. Tom's ideals seem unrealistic to May, although she can appreciate that he has his own life a head of him and appears to believe that he is throwing away his future by enlisting.

Ralph and Eva have only been seeing each other for a few months. Theirs is a more stereotypical relationship, with Eva worrying that Ralph will forget all about her. She feels unsure about her future once he has gone. Ralph, on the other hand, cheats on Eva, sleeping with prostitutes while in France. Although he feels guilty about this, one senses that he misses the physical side of their relationship more than anything else.

Another stereotypical couple can be seen in Annie and Arthur Boggis. Annie seems to rule their household with a rod of iron and has barely a good word to say about either her husband or her son. Once the pigeon appears and Annie believes Arthur to be dead, she falls apart, becoming hysterical and clinging to Reggie for support. This seems a strange reaction from someone who had appeared not to care a great deal about her husband and there could be more than one explanation for this. It may be that her behaviour prior to Arthur's death was a fabrication and, although she may not have loved him greatly, it is perfectly possible that she did care for him, but found it necessary, for some reason, to pretend otherwise. This may have been because she preferred her neighbours to see her as a hard character, with no feelings for others. Alternatively, an explanation for her breakdown could be her concern for herself and Reggie now that Arthur is dead. They are a poor family and the loss of her husband, even though she and Reggie work, would have a huge impact on their finances and their future.

Another relationship which bears some scrutiny is that between May and Eva. Despite a faltering beginning, caused by Tom neglecting to mention Eva's arrival, the two women soon form a friendship. May has a reputation among her neighbours for her high expectations and desire to better herself. Eva, being fair-minded, refuses to judge her new friend, showing loyalty towards May, who has given her a job and a roof over her head. She remains grateful to May, even when the older woman asks her to perform tasks which she is really unwilling to undertake, such as singing at the charity concert. May clearly trusts Eva and offers to make her a partner in her new business venture. Eva's scepticism about May's motives demonstrates her ability to understand May's real feelings, as she believes that May really hopes that Eva's presence will entice Ralph and, therefore, Tom to join the two women. Although May denies this accusation, it is clear that Eva has offended May and this episode marks the beginning of the end of their close friendship. Despite this, the audience know that May's feelings for Tom are stronger than she will admit and it is possible that she becomes angry with Eva because the younger girl has managed to see through May's defences.

COMPARISONS

EFFECTS OF THE WAR

In common with a great deal of other literature about the First World War, *The Accrington Pals* demonstrates how people reacted in different ways to various events during the war. In most cases, these reactions reflect the impact of the war on each individual, rather than its effects on the general population. May, for example, is torn between anger at Tom for enlisting and taking advantage of her newly discovered business opportunities. Tom, on the other hand, initially sees it as his duty to enlist and, once in the army, he is impressed by the efficiency and methods employed.

Unlike much of the other literature of the First World War, the effects of the war in *The Accrington Pals* are shown from the perspective of those left behind. This is mainly because of the unique nature of the Pals' involvment in the war and the realisation that such high casualties would have a profound impact on the areas involved. *The Return of the Soldier* by Rebecca West is another 'home-front' piece. In this novel, the hero, Chris Baldry has lost his memory and returns to his home still believing that he is in a relationship with his first love Margaret. He has no memory of his wife Kitty. The dilemma which faces these two women, and Chris's cousin Jenny is whether to return Chris to 'normal' and let him go back to the dangers of the war, or to keep him safe at home, living a false life. No such problems exist in the lives of the women in *The Accrington Pals*: their concerns are for how they will exist without their men. These two pieces go to demonstrate that the impact of the war on the individuals at home depended entirely upon their direct involvement, their class, their social and financial status and their relationship with the person they have lost.

In *The Accrington Pals*, as the war progresses, the people at home still continue to hold out hopes that the latest 'big push' will be the one to end the conflict. This portrayal of home-front complacency and its effects of giving unrealistically high-hopes, is the sort of reaction which angered many serving soldiers, especially some of the poets. Siegfried Sassoon was probably the most vociferous of these and frequently wrote poems which expressed his feelings of injustice and bitterness towards those at home, who continued to believe the 'lies'. Among these are *Glory of Women, Does it Matter?* and *Suicide in the Trenches*, all of which demonstrate the difference between the reality of the solider's life and experiences and the portrayal of those experiences at home.

Eventually, some of the characters are seen to face up to the death of a loved-one and the audience witnesses the effect that this has upon their lives and personalities. The scale of losses in *The Accrington Pals* makes the impact of the deaths of the men much more forceful. The women initially believe that only seven men have survived, so all must face the stark reality of loss. However, their new-found independence makes them question the newspaper reports and they march on the town hall to discover the truth. The need for those at home to discover the truth about the men they have lost was a common reality. Many families would write to senior officers and the war office, desperate for news of loved-ones, or to discover the real facts behind a death. An example of this can be seen in *Strange Meeting* by Susan Hill, when David Barton's mother writes to John Hilliard, desperate for news of her son. All too often the information which families were able to glean was sketchy or incomplete. In fact, Rudyard Kipling, whose son John was killed on 27th September 1915 at the Battle of Loos, spent the rest of his life trying to discover the events which had led up to his son's death and the whereabouts of his body.

PORTRAYAL OF WOMEN

Much of the literature of the First World War leaves out the role of women altogether. In other pieces, women are portrayed less flatteringly than their male counterparts. This is not the case in *The Accrington Pals*. May, for example, while always independently seeking to better herself and leave the slums behind her, is also seen to be quietly kind-hearted. This 'roundness' of character can also be seen in Sarah Lumb, the central female character in Pat Barker's novel *Regeneration*. Sarah has a working-class background, works in a munitions factory and is fiercely independent. Her character, like many of those in *The Accrington Pals*, reflects the changes women were undergoing in the course of the war: active participation in the war effort, rather than a subservient role in society. At the same time, however, Sarah demonstrates her feelings of injustice towards the conflict. When she speaks of her dead boyfriend, she is angry that it was British gas which killed him. Equally, when she visits the hospital, she resents the maimed men being hidden away from the public - believing that a nation which expects its young men to give so much, should at least have the decency to face the consequences.

All of the female characters in *The Accrington Pals* have strong personalities, they say what they think and are not necessarily prepared to believe everything they are told. Their roles change as the war progresses and this is reflected by most of the female characters taking on additional or different work to help in the war effort. The changing role of working women during the First World War is also portrayed in Jessie Pope's poem *War Girls*, in which she describes the various tasks undertaken by women and their loyalty to both their men and their country. As with most of her work, Pope's portrayal is idealistic, although there is an element of reality in this poem, as shown in *The Accrington Pals*. The suggestion in both of these pieces is that, regardless of what happens to their men, the role of women in society has changed.

Many of the other women, with the obvious exception of Eva, are not sorry to see their men go and fight and seem to think it only right that they should have joined up. Bertha's reaction to the attentions of a young man who has failed his medical examination are noteworthy. Although he cannot help his illness, Bertha seems to think there would be an element of shame attached to marrying, or even loving him. This attitude is also reflected in the play *Oh What a Lovely War*, where women are portrayed as goading men into enlisting and showing contempt for those who refuse. This latter play, however, provides a stereotypical account of the First World War, as seen from the 1960s. *The Accrington Pals* would seem, therefore, to give a more realistic portrayal, showing many different reactions, based as much on individual personalities and relationships as on a general train of thought.

The women in *The Accrington Pals* are shown to be much more involved in the war effort and the lives of their menfolk than many other female characters in First World War literature. These women, with a few exceptions, show their emotions and are not afraid of demonstrating their feelings for others. Many authors frequently portray women as unfeeling or aloof from the circumstances which are unravelling around them. Kitty in *The Return of the Soldier* by Rebecca West is shown to be a selfish, uncaring woman who refuses to let the war have any impact on her lifestyle or existence. When her husband returns to her unaware, due to amnesia, that they are even married, her sole concern is how this event will impact on her life and social status. She shows no concern for her husband's future wellbeing, but is merely anxious to regain her pre-war life. Equally, the character of Constance Hilliard in Susan Hill's *Strange Meeting* is emotionally constrained, never revealing her feelings to her son, despite the losses he suffers during the war. She is a woman who is incapable of showing emotion, keeping her feelings, if she has any, firmly to herself. It could be argued, however, that these differences are as much to do with class and social status as anything else. Both Kitty and Constance are upper-class ladies, who have probably been raised to believe that it is a weakness to show one's feelings. The women in *The Accrington Pals* have no such scruples - how their demonstrations of emotion are perceived is unimportant to them.

FAITH

Faith, including the loss of it, is a common theme in First World War literature, with many authors examining the role of religious beliefs during the conflict. This can take the form of characters discovering, maintaining or losing their belief in God. A change of beliefs at such a time is hardly surprising or unreasonable. The vast majority of soldiers were being placed in situations they had never experienced before and some of the events they witnessed were enough to make anyone question their previously held convictions. For some, the prospect of their own impending death made them more ready to turn to God for guidance, while others, who may previously have held strong beliefs, began to question God's role in the carnage they were enduring.

In *The Accrington Pals*, Arthur Boggis is clearly a religious man and, in his very first appearance, the conversation rapidly turns to God. In fact, his speeches always revolve around his beliefs. Prior to his departure, he says a prayer to the assembled company. The others join in, except Tom, who seems to follow no religion. Arthur's letter to his friend Jack explains his feelings about the war and his belief that he is doing God's work. He asserts that it is man's failure to live by God's laws that have brought about the conflict and that this is His way of purifying the world of its sins. However, this letter is written while Arthur is still in training and once he is in the trenches, his outlook changes. When CSM Rivers suggests that Arthur say a prayer before they go over-the-top, Arthur's response is to sarcastically ask God if he finds their situation pleasing. His experiences and the sights he has witness have clearly affected his beliefs. This change of heart is confirmed by CSM Rivers when he tells May that Arthur had denied his God before he died. In common with others, Arthur's experiences have made him question how his God could allow such atrocities to take place: how He could allow such suffering.

This is echoed in *Birdsong* by Sebastian Faulks. In this novel, the character Jack Firebrace, like Arthur Boggis, has a long-standing and deep-rooted belief in God. As the story progresses, Jack's faith is continually tested. Firstly his young son becomes seriously ill and then, despite Jack's prayers, the boy dies. Although some might believe, at such a time, that they had been let down by their God, Jack's faith remains intact. In fact, he writes to his grieving wife at home and tells her that they should be grateful to God for allowing them the opportunity of knowing their wonderful son. However, on 1st July 1916, everything changes. Jack, as a tunneller is not one of the soldiers going over-the-top. Instead he and his friend, together with the Padré stand behind the lines, and from their vantage point, they witness the carnage of the first day of the Battle of the Somme. The massacre unfolding before them leaves these men altered: Arthur Shaw, Jack's friend - a strong, burly miner, cries like a baby; the Padré, Horrocks, throws away his silver cross in disgust, unable to believe the sights he is witnessing. Jack, meanwhile, knows and silently accepts that his belief in God has gone forever.

A Question of Comparisons

Many students have to make direct comparisons between two particular texts, demonstrating the author's treatment of a specific topic. Where this is dealt with as coursework, some examination boards allow that the student may be permitted to choose the texts for themselves. To that end, we have included a list of possible topics and suggested texts which, in our opinion, provide suitable material for such essays, assuming that *The Accrington Pals* will be one of the texts involved. What follows below is not a series of 'answers' because in this situation, it is for each student to decide what to include and how they wish to study each piece in question. Instead, this section is meant to whet the appetite: to give students a point from which to start in making their own comparisons.

THE CHANGING ROLE OF WOMEN

Quite often in the literature of the First World War, the role of women is minimalised, or even non-existant. *The Accrington Pals* is a notable exception to this, providing ample examples of the way in which women were forced to change their lives as a result of the conflict.

Using The Accrington Pals and Regeneration

The women in both of these pieces are working-class, independent and strong. Students could choose to focus either on the general role of women as portrayed in these two works, or take particular characters and study their personalities and lives more closely.

For example, although Sarah Lumb in *Regeneration* and May Hassal in *The Accrington Pals* both work, Sarah works in a munitions factory, aware that she has a responsibility to 'do her bit' for the war effort. May, on the other hand, runs her own business and is always looking for ways to improve both it and herself. However, Sarah's outlook is not entirely selfless as she chose to work in the munitions factory rather than be a servant - the pay is better, but also she resents the idea of being subservient. Both women have adapted well to their situations:

May's strong independence stands her in good stead, while Sarah's quick mind and forceful character ensure that nobody will get the better of her. Both Sarah and May are slow to show their emotions - neither one really prepared to commit themselves to the men who claim to love them.

Students who choose to focus on the general representation of the role of women within these pieces could look at the language which both authors have used. The women in both pieces often meet together outside of their workplaces. Their discussions focus on the men in their lives; their working conditions; occasionally the war and their friendships with each other. Their language is invariably coarse or masculine, showing their down-to-earth nature.

PORTRAYAL OF FRIENDSHIPS IN WAR

Many pieces of First World War literature, both poetry and prose, look at the friendships formed during the war. Usually, these friendships concern men who meet as a consequence of the war, but there is no reason why students could not choose to compare these friendships with those formed by the women left behind.

Using The Accrington Pals and Journey's End

The friendships in *The Accrington Pals* - with the exception of that between Tom and Ralph - are between women. They all work or live in close proximity and share the similar fate of having their menfolk go off to fight in the war. This circumstance brings them all much closer together, ensuring a common bond and a strength of friendship which is, probably, new to these women. Although their lives are less harsh or dangerous than the men's, they still have the daily hardships of working-class life to contend with - except that now they are alone. They also have to deal with their fears about their men not returning and what will happen to them in that event. The women have differing opinions on many matters, such as whether or not the men should have joined up in the first place, but the audience is left with the impression that, ultimately, these women will remain bound together in their grief and hardship.

Journey's End, on the other hand, is about a group of soldiers, thrown together in a dug-out in the spring of 1918. These men know that an attack is about to take place and that there is every chance that they will not all survive. In the short time that the audience spends with them, it becomes clear that these men have become like a close-knit family unit. They must remain loyal to each other in order to fight at their best. They also understand that their relationships with one another are probably the strongest that they will experience in their lives.

Students who choose to study these two plays in this way should pay attention to the social class of the two sets of people involved: *Journey's End* concerns officers - most of whom are upper or middle class; *The Accrington Pals* has a working class setting. This means that the characters will react to their situations differently, but it is interesting to note that both sets of poeple show an element of reserve in their emotional reactions.

Further Reading

To the Last Man: Spring 1918
by Lyn MacDonald

As with all of Lyn MacDonald's excellent books, To the Last Man tells its story through the words of the people who were there. It is not restricted to a British perspective, but tells of the first few months of 1918 and their momentous consequences from every angle. The author gives just the right amount of background information of a political and historical nature to keep the reader interested and informed, while leaving the centre-stage to those who really matter... the men themselves. This is an invaluable book for anyone studying Journey's End as it helps, probably more than any other book, in the understanding of the personalities involved and the time through which they were living.

Strange Meeting
by Susan Hill

Strange Meeting is a beautiful and moving book. It is the story of two young men, who meet in the worst circumstances, yet manage to overcome their surroundings and form a deep and lasting friendship. Susan Hill writes so evocatively that the reader is automatically drawn into the lives of these men: the sights, sounds and even smells which they witness are brought to life. It is a book about war and its effects; it is also a story of love, both conventional and 'forbidden'; of human relationships of every variety. This is a tale told during the worst of times, about the best of men.

Not About Heroes
by Stephen MacDonald

Probably one of the most underrated First World War plays, this details the meeting between Wilfred Owen and Siegfried Sassoon. It is a humourous, tragic and above all, moving account of this friendship and is based on diary entries and extracts from autobiographies.

The Complete Memoirs of George Sherston
by Siegfried Sassoon

An autobiographical account of Sassoon's life before and during the First World War. Sassoon has changed the names of the characters and George Sherston (Sassoon) is not a poet. This trilogy (made up of Memoirs of a Fox Hunting Man, Memoirs of an Infantry Officer and Sherston's Progress) demonstrates the effects of the war on both the serving soldiers and those left at home.

For a list of the fictional characters and their factual counterparts, see Appendix II of **Siegfried Sassoon** *by John Stuart Roberts*.

The Return of the Soldier
by Rebecca West

Written in 1918, this home-front novel gives a useful insight into the trauma of war, as seen through the eyes of three women. Chris Baldry, an officer and husband of Kitty, returns home suffering from shell-shock and amnesia, believing that he is still in a relationship with Margaret Allington - his first love. Kitty, Margaret and Chris's cousin, Jenny, must decide whether to leave Chris in his make-believe world, safe from the war; or whether to 'cure' him and risk his future welfare once he returns to being a soldier.

All Quiet on the Western Front
by Erich Maria Remarque

Written from first-hand experience of life in the trenches, this novel is the moving account of the lives of a group of young German soldiers during the First World War. The fact that this, often shocking, story is told from a German perspective demonstrates the universal horrors of the war and the sympathy between men of both sides for others enduring the same hardships as themselves.

Bibliography

The First World War
by John Keegan

Chronology of the Great War, 1914-1918
Edited by Lord Edward Gleichen

Journey's End
by R C Sherriff

Regeneration
by Pat Barker

Birdsong
by Sebastian Faulks

The Return of the Soldier
by Rebecca West

The Accrington Pals
by Peter Whelan

Pals on the Somme 1916
by Roni Wilkinson

The Somme
by Peter Hart

British Culture and the First World War
by George Robb

Other Titles

GREAT WAR LITERATURE STUDY GUIDE E-BOOKS:
NOVELS & PLAYS

All Quiet on the Western Front
Birdsong
Journey's End (A-Level or GCSE)
Regeneration
The Eye in the Door
The Ghost Road
A Long Long Way
The First Casualty
Strange Meeting
The Return of the Soldier
The Accrington Pals
Not About Heroes
Oh What a Lovely War

POET BIOGRAPHIES AND POETRY ANALYSIS:

Herbert Asquith
Harold Begbie
John Peale Bishop
Edmund Blunden
Vera Brittain
Rupert Brooke
Thomas Burke
May Wedderburn Cannan
Margaret Postgate Cole
Alice Corbin
E E Cummings

Nancy Cunard
T S Eliot
Eleanor Farjeon
Gilbert Frankau
Robert Frost
Wilfrid Wilson Gibson
Anna Gordon Keown
Robert Graves
Julian Grenfell
Ivor Gurney
Thomas Hardy
Alan P Herbert
Agnes Grozier Herbertson
W N Hodgson
A E Housman
Geoffrey Anketell Studdert Kennedy
Winifred M Letts
Amy Lowell
E A Mackintosh
John McCrae
Charlotte Mew
Edna St Vincent Millay
Ruth Comfort Mitchell
Harriet Monroe
Edith Nesbit
Robert Nichols
Wilfred Owen
Jessie Pope
Ezra Pound
Florence Ripley Mastin
Isaac Rosenberg
Carl Sandburg
Siegfried Sassoon
Alan Seeger
Charles Hamilton Sorley
Wallace Stevens
Sara Teasdale
Edward Wyndham Tennant
Lesbia Thanet
Edward Thomas

Iris Tree
Katharine Tynan Hinkson
Robert Ernest Vernède
Arthur Graeme West

Please note that e-books are only available direct from our Web site at www.greatwarliterature.co.uk and cannot be purchased through bookshops.

NOTES

Printed in Dunstable, United Kingdom